PHANTOM OF THE DUMP: NO CORONA HERE

A FANCIFUL FARCE IN THREE ACTS

~

Phantom of the Dump: No Corona Here

A Fanciful Farce in Three Acts

~

Joseph A. Bonelli

SUNSTONE PRESS

SANTA FE

Sunstone books may be purchased for educational, business, or sales promotional use.
For information please write: Special Markets Department, Sunstone Press,
P.O. Box 2321, Santa Fe, New Mexico 87504-2321.
Printed on acid-free paper
∞

———————————————————

Library of Congress Cataloging-in-Publication Data

Names: Bonelli, Joseph A., 1942- author.
Title: Phantom of the dump: no Corona here : a fanciful farce in three acts
  / Joseph A. Bonelli.
Description: Santa Fe : Sunstone Press, [2023] | Summary: "A comedy about
  good people and zanies: Chief Joseph (Town Council); Mayor Shorty; Sally
  Jones, barmaid and proprietress of the Dogpatch Saloon, aka Stupifyin
  Jones; and Prospector Mike and his burro Hillary (not that Hillary!)"--
  Provided by publisher.
Identifiers: LCCN 2023034905 | ISBN 9781632935496 (paperback) | ISBN
  9781611397239 (epub)
Subjects: LCGFT: Comedy plays.
Classification: LCC PS3602.O657156 P47 2023 | DDC 812.6--dc23/
eng/20230803
LC record available at https://lccn.loc.gov/2023034905

———————————————————

WWW.SUNSTONEPRESS.COM
SUNSTONE PRESS / POST OFFICE BOX 2321 / SANTA FE, NM 87504-2321 /USA
(505) 988-4418

N.B. If you don't like to laugh, stop reading now. Go read something sad and tragic. Like Sophocles. Or the daily newspaper.

PHANTOM OF THE DUMP:
NO CORONA HERE

It all takes place in the mythical town of Snowtop in the mythical county of Winchester, in the real cold state of Washington. Starting as a light-hearted parody of "Phantom of the Opera," it evolved (taking the writer with it) into a paean to the current day Old West. The Old West still lives out there in its descendants in small, rural western towns; modern towns now but still Mark Twain and Louis L'Amour country at heart. Towns where they have Corona beer but no Corona virus of any kind...until they let in the tourists.

The people are cowboys, ranchers, sheepmen, nesters, and merchants all living together in the shadow of towering mountains and burning deserts in the clean mountain air under a canopy of stars. All working hard to eke out a subsistence living but helping each other out in the tiny Snowtop valley. Snowtop is located at the end of Dylan Highway 61. Its leaders rotate the mayor's gavel on a yearly basis and short straw is "it" for the next year.

The "Phantom" is a monster surprised by Gary Gardiano, the Town Dumpmaster, and his junkyard dog, Bowser, eating garbage in the municipal dump and cemetery. The garbage turns out to be a Columbian drug dealer with ties to Al Quaeda so the DEA and the FBI come to town. They are followed by CNN and other media. The investigation leads to the red dust of a Witch Mountain mine where the FBI agents, Tiffany and Chester, and the DEA Agent Walter O'Rourke, shoot it out with a kooky drug gang known as the Loko Mokos. Collateral damage includes a collapse of the mine tunnel and discovery of new ore veins.

The town's leaders include Mayor Shorty, an ex-English teacher,

Sally Jones (aka Stupifyin' Jones), proprietress and barmaid of the Dogpatch Saloon, and Mabel Stokely, member of the Town Council, Postmistress, and Justice of the Peace.

Chief Joseph (Nez Perce) is the town's biologist and tracker who identifies the prints at the dump as those of a "Wallamootka" (a wolverine) and predicts it will likely return in approximately eight days on its "Paper Route." It does this on Earth Day! An omen.

Opportunities open up and the town adds Ecotourism to their economic base in a dispute with the Federales over the identity and proper burying of the CORPSE. Notoriety brings tourists and strangers to town including a wannabe vampire who wants a tour guide to take him to Hidden Valley, a remote location where there was a rodent outbreak of Bubonic Plague in 01. Corona virus hovers but does not land. Other strangers include brave wolf hunters who are not welcome in a town devoted to ecotourism.

Mrs. Guerrero and her daughter visit, and after finding out that Mr. G's corpse was honorably cared for, they endow a city park and a bronze statue of a Wallamootka.

Sally and Charley get hitched and Sally reopens her grandad's old-fashioned hand work gold mine. With this, "The Great Depression" that began in 1929 finally ends for Snowtop. The city pulls itself up by the bootstraps into the 21st century. Yippee! Here we come!

DRAMATIS PERSONAE

~

Gary Gardiano: Master of the Snowtop Municipal Dump and Cemetery. Young, smart, and earnest; he will go far

Bowser: His dutiful but cheeky dog friend

The Phantom: A Wallamootka (Old Mandan dialect)

Mayor Shorty: A retired English teacher and mayor of the tiny town of Snowtop, Washington

Chief Joseph: Member of the Town Council, great-great-grandson of THE Chief Joseph, and local cattle and sheep rancher

Mabel Stokely: Member of the Town Council and co-owner of the Snowtop Bakery and General Store. Post-mistress and Justice of the Peace. Unretired senior citizen

Herbert Stokely: Runs bakery and general store. Makes terrific "bear sign" (cowboy donuts); keeps wife Mabel from running in circles

Sally Jones: Barmaid and Proprietress of the Dogpatch Saloon, Snowtop's only eatery and boozery; aka Stupifyin Jones

Phil Fenton: Chief of Police

Trooper Murphy: Washington State Highway Patrol Officer

Walter O'Rourke: DEA Agent, human being, middle-aged, smart and sassy

Tiffany Gates: FBI Agent, young, intelligent, attractive, and still idealistic

Chester Detweiler: FBI Agent, tall handsome, conciliatory, but not too bright

Charley Cruikshank: Attorney, Snowtop's legal counsel, and town schoolmaster

Mohammed El Rashid bin Laden Guerrero: THE CORPSE

Senora Guerrero: The Corpse's Wife, gorgeous but dangerous.

Senorita Guerrero: The Corpse's Daughter, young, beautiful, multitalented, multilingual

Margo Bernstein: Snowtop Hotel Manageress

Clyde Fosdick: Fearless Wolf Hunter

Prospector Mike: Old and still looking for gold

Milt Hartley: CNN Talking Head

Santini: Helicopter Pilot

Chorus: One or more persons, onstage or backstage (director's choice)

ACT 1, SCENE 1

(Shack at the Entrance to the Snowtop Municipal Dump and Cemetery. "Kilroy Was Here – 1872" is spray-painted across the front. Present are Gary and Bowser. 4:30 a.m.)

Gary

GUARDIAN! That's what I am. Gary Gardiano is my moniker for those of you who need labels to tack people down. Guardian of the garbage dump am I, of the incorporated town of Snowtop, in the ice cold state of Washington. Not to be confused with that other Washington. That swamp place. I'm paid to see that no one molests our garbage. Thought I heard a noise. Don't usually get up this early.

Bowser

Bow Wow!

Gary

I run the municipal dump by day and guard the garbage by night. What a crock! Ever hear of anybody stealing garbage? Course, I'm sposed to keep people from leaving their garbage here after hours. No Arlo Guthries wanted here please. The Dump Annex houses our municipal cemetery. I'm in charge of that too, but since I don't have to dig graves, it's light duty. Don't bury more than one or two people a year here unless there's a bad accident on Dylan Highway 61.

(Sound effects: Car crash and chorus is heard moaning.)

Chorus

HEAR! HEAR! Hear the voice of the Night Guardian!
Keeper of the sludge. Lord of the flies. Recyclero Supremo!
Garbachero Gargantuo. Guardian of the GRAVES! Son of
Anubis, Protector of the dead.

Gary

Spooky wind out there tonight! My town council is so
cheap, their municipal retirement plan is a Greyhound
bus ticket to the Social Security out-station in Winchester,
our county seat, forty-three miles down that road over there.
Highway 61, the one that goes up through the high mountain
passes. If you retire in winter, they have to spring, pardon
the pun, for a heftier fare around the long way—that's a
hundred and twenty-two miles! Unless you want to reinvent
the Donner Party's mistake.

Bowser

Bow wow!

Gary

Hey, Little Dude, how's it hanging? I'm busy orating
here. Hardly anyone in this town is paid the minimum
wage either. Just the lawyer, the doc, the police chief,
and the nurse at the clinic. Hey! I'm not complaining.
Happy to have any job around here. I've got my high
school diploma—even earned it; didn't buy it like some
people I won't name. Think we suffered from the 07
recession? Nuts! People here don't even know the
Great Depression is over. When the town runs out of
money they pay my salary in credit chits to the
General Store or Sally's. No deficit financing here.

Bowser

Bow wow WOW!

Gary

What you want Dog? I'm talking here. You know it's
bad manners to interrupt.

Bowser

(getting up from all fours, he addresses the audience)
It's bad manners to bore people too, esteemed Bossman.
He had a can of pork and beans for dinner and now he's
full of it. I always stay upwind of him when he's had this
particular dinner. Sounds like one of those windy DC
politicians.

(Bowser goes back on all fours)

Gary

Those weenies in Washington preach economic
development and diversification but don't tell us how.
The county unemployment rate is 37.37 percent and our
only local criminal, a burglar, has to commute to the next
county south of us. There hasn't been a single job created
in Snowtop since 2007. Do the math! And we ain't seen any of
that there Corona bailout money neither. Course we ain't
seen any Corona either,'cept in a bottle over at the
Dogpatch Saloon.

Bowser

BOW WOW!

Gary

The county only has 997 people and our town has...

Chorus

Enough! Enough! Listen to your dog. The audience don't
want no pinko civics lecture. On with the evil and the gore!
Ever more. There is evil afoot tonight.

Bowser

WOOF! WOOF!

Gary

YIKES! Bowser, what you up to dog? You scared me out
of two years growth.

Bowser

WOOF! WOOF!

(Bowser gets up from all fours and turns to the audience)

Bowser

There's a wolf out there, dummy. Been trying to tell you
but you don't understand English. Well, I think it's a wolf.
Real gamey and macho like. Never smelled one before, I'm
a town dog, not Yukon King. And Gary's no Sergeant
Preston either, but he gives a good tummy rub and ear scratch.

(Goes back down on all fours)

The Phantom (offstage)

AUURGH! GLOP! SLOP! MURF! WOP!

Gary

Holy Canole! What's that? Look over there, Bowser.

Bowser

WOOF! WOOF!

(Bowser jumps back on two feet)

Bowser (continues)

Gee, I hate repeating myself. Gary can be dumb as dogshit
sometimes. I miss Dr. Dolittle.

Gary

Bowser, stay on guard, I've got to get a flashlight.

Bowser

Yo Captain! Hey dummy, bring your shotgun too.

Gary shines flashlight. Sees two luminous eyes and hears
a loud growl as the phantom abruptly disappears. An
upswelling of eerie Bach organ music is followed by the
swirl of Scottish pipes, howling of wolves, then the yipping
of a single crazed coyote.)

CHORUS
HEAR! HEAR! Thus begins the music of the night! The
restless spirits, like Riders of the Storm, hail the coming
of a demon from hell—a terror from the land of Cthulu
and the Plains of Azusa—to haunt the quiet Snowtop Valley.

(Chorus howls like wolves)

Gary
What the Sam Hill was that? Feral dog or coyote it was not.
It could have eaten one of those guys for breakfast.
Couldn't have been a wolf either, they never come near
town. Yuck, it was right by the cemetery. Ghouls are
are not good for real estate values. Bowser! Bowser,
where are you? I need your company and your nose.

(Finds Bowser under his cot. Puts a leash on him.)

Gary
Man up, little hairy dude. You're supposed to act like
Snoopy, not Beetle Bailey. Let's go Tiger.

Bowser
MEOW!

(They walk over to where the phantom had appeared.)

Gary
Holy Hannah, this can't be happening to me. Gotta get to the
phone, or maybe I should puke first.

(Runs to the shack, dragging Bowser who carries a bone.)

Gary (continues)

Bowser, drop that bone you klunkhead. You're destroying evidence of a crime.

(Music plays Dragnet theme or opening bars of Beethoven's Fifth.)

Chief of Police Fenton

(answering phone offstage)

Good evening. Snowtop Police Department. How can I help you?

Gary

Cut the cute, Phil. This is Gary at the dump. Get over here right away. You have a body to investigate. And I have to puke. Maybe.

(Gary turns toward audience)

Gary

Hey, you out there! Why do bad things happen to good people?

(Siren is heard and Chief Fenton rushes in.)

Chief Fenton

Gary, you nervous nerd. Slow down. You know the slaughterhouse sometimes sends you cow carcasses. And Hillary's been missing for a week!

Gary

Phil, this is not Prospector Mike's burro Hillary. This cow's wearing a three piece suit, his face cheeks have been ripped away and he's full of gold dental work. His other cheeks are, like gone. That's not the bad part.

Chief Fenton

It isn't? Tell me the rest of it.

Gary

There's a gruesome monster here dude. He was, like feeding on this guy. The corpse is a glucky mess and he's missing a leg. Wait, I think Bowser was chewing on that leg. His head looks like Dirty Harry was using it for target practice. Huge feet too, size thirteen, and he's got six toes on the foot that's still attached.

Chief Fenton

Gary, you been chewing Jimson weed?

Gary

Never touch the stuff dude. You know me. Ain't nobody in this town has a criminal record except YOU-KNOW-WHO.

Chief Fenton

Now don't trash...YOU-KNOW-WHO, he's a county tax payer, of which we don't have many. He's keeping his nose clean.

Gary

Chief, get focused dude, you got terrible trouble here.

Chief Fenton

Damn! I've got to call in the State Police on this one if half of what Gary says is true. My horoscope didn't warn me about today. Think I'll mail in a complaint. First, I better check out this creepy corpse to make sure Gary isn't hallucinating. Can't tell about folks these days with all the legal grass around. I hate to think Gary is a contestant in our yearly Labor Day 'spin a whopper tall tale' contest in honor of Mark Twain, and he's trying out his spiel on me early.

(He exits.)

ACT 1, SCENE 2

(Mayor Shorty's Office, 7 a.m. Furnishings are old-fashioned, rustic, and simple. Lots of chairs. Town meetings are held here as are non-sectarian religious services. Present are Trooper Murphy and Chief Fenton)

Chief Fenton
So Murphy, where's your forensic people on this one?
All you did up there at the dump was cover the carcass
with a tarp and talk on your cellular. And eat my donut
and burp.

Trooper Murphy
They're coming, Phil. But it ain't my state guys, it's
the Feds.

(Music Plays. Several bars of the William Tell overture)

Chief Fenton
Feds! They don't have any jurisdiction here! Why the
devil do they want in on this? We're no Indian reservation.

Trooper Murphy
It's like this, Phil. When getting ready to phone our guys,
I joked about "Goldtooth" and his six toes. One of our
secretaries is balling a DEA guy and she suddenly
sounded sick and started screaming on the telephone.

Seems DEA has been looking for Goldtooth around these parts; he's a big boy in the drug trade. He also has terrorist connections, so Homeland Security is interested. DEA and FBI will be here in about 7 minutes. They're 99% sure they know who our corpse is.

Chief Fenton
Holy Toledo! I better get next door to the bakery and get some donuts and coffee. And warn Herby to start some more batter and grinds.

Trooper Murphy
And that three-day-old donut you gave me was pretty good, thanks. Pure congealed sugar falling into a well of gastric juices.

Chief Fenton
You're welcome. Anytime, buddy.

ACT 1, SCENE 3

(Mayor Shorty's office, 11:30 a.m., same day. Present are the Mayor, FBI Agents (Chester and Tiffany) and DEA Agent Walter, State Trooper Murphy, Chief Fenton, and Chief Joseph. Chief Joseph wears jeans, cowboy boots, red flannel shirt, and a beaded headband with wolf drawings, and a single eagle feather.)

Chester
Mayor Shorty, who's that Indian? He doesn't belong in this meeting. Or does he?

Mayor Shorty
At ease, big guy. Chief Joseph is a member of the Town Council; along with Mabel and Herb. They're busy next door cooking donuts and grinding coffee. One of them will join us soon.

Chester
I've heard of this Chief Joseph guy.

Mayor Shorty
Nah, that was his great-great-grandfather. But bear in mind
there's lots of folks round here with Nez Perce blood. Don't
like to advertise it in case the Army is still looking for them.
A few of Joseph's band got to Canada; some of 'em
snuck down to Snowtop in the spring of 1878. And
stayed. Back to basics, gentlemen. We have a monster
loose in this community. What are you going to do about it?

Tiffany
Nothing. That's your problem. We have a positive make on
Mohammed El Rashid bin Laden Guerrero. We're interested
in how he got in your dump and who offed him, but you can
deal with your monster yourself. We know he or she didn't
do it. One of Mohammed's toes was chewed off and his foot
mangled. Our science team is thinking the body was buried
in the dump with only one toe showing. Your monster yanked
him out of there by that foot. But he was already way dead
before then. Sloppy job of burying him. It's hard to get good
help these days even in their business where the pay is so good.

Chester
They got good retirement benefits too, I hear, but no one lives
long enough to collect them. Ha! Ha!

Chief Fenton
Hey, don't joke about that. We got no retirement benefits here.

Mayor Shorty
Have you guys got any clue why this Mohammed character
is buried in our dump? Who hated him enough to go to all
the trouble of dumping him here after he was already a
bullet-riddled corpse?

Walter
Actually, we haven't the foggiest who or why someone
would do that. Course he had competitors, but no one into
kinky stuff like burying him in a public dump. If he had a
wooden stake in his heart or a silver crossbow bolt up his
butt, we would have more to go on.

Chester
Way I hear it every male in this county owns a shotgun and
drives a pickup. Shouldn't be any trouble for ya to take care
of one little ole monster.

Mayor Shorty
You guys are cheap. So who is this Mohammed character?

Tiffany
He's a Columbian drug lord like his father before him. His
wife was a Saudi Arabian princess, cousin of bin Laden, who
emigrated under suspicious circumstances. We suspect
Mohammed had some kind of drug pipeline around here,
funneling drugs from Canada. His clothes all had red dust
in every pocket crevice so we figure he had been buried
once already.

Chief Joseph
So you think he might have been pre-buried in Utah or Vegas?
Poor schmuck. Twice buried and resurrected to be munched on
by a ghoul. I call that real mala suerte.

Chester
Malawho?

Chief Joseph
Bad luck. Say, about that red dust, there's a small outcrop of
Navajo Sandstone on the south side of Witch Mountain. Maybe...

Chester

Guys! Guys! Listen a minute. The mayor is right. We have to find out about this monster—and maybe even take him out. It's proper investigative protocol. Never know, it might give us a clue we need.

(Music plays William Tell Overture)

Mayor Shorty
Wait a minute gents. If you say this guy was pre-buried before coming to stay with us, you just have to find out why. Makes no sense. We don't want no precedent or something. Have to think of our reputation.

(Mabel Stokely enters room waving computer printout sheets and carrying a box.)

Mabel
Your attention please, Gentlemen. We're in the news!

Mayor Shorty
What news Mabel?

Mabel
The National Enquirer, the Winchester Weekly, and CNN! CNN is sending a TV team as we speak, and we don't have a single hotel or motel room in town. Triple A maps don't even show this town.

Mayor Shorty
Quick, Mabel. Call Margo and tell her to open up some of the street side rooms in the boarded-up parts of Hotel Snowtop. We'll give her a temporary business license by noon if she gets Virgil's dogs in there to clean out the rats, and a clean-up crew from Sally's.

Mabel
Will do, Mayor.

Mayor Shorty
Gents, the core of the hotel is already operational for a
couple of long-term tenants so if you decide to stay
tonight, you'll have all the amenities.

Mabel
Gentlemen, there's fresh donuts next door. We'll even
deliver if you know what sugar-honey you want. Our
specialty de la maison is Huckleberry creams, Jelly
Whompers and just plain Sugar Daddies. Have some
samples right here. And if you need postal services
they're right next door in our Bakery/General Store.

(Mabel exits)

(Music plays. Ride of the Valkyries)

(Chomp! Chomp, Slurp, Slurp. Everybody is eating the donuts.)

CHORUS
(In rap cadence or rhythm or clapping)
Bad dude man go deep down/in de ground/where red dust
rule/in mean ass school/didn't know the rule/watch yo
back, man. It comin. Dig on de night/music shinin bright/
at midnight/voices outa sight/music dat ain't right/ Heavy
Man! Heavy!

Chester
Mayor Shorty, you guys have real spooky winds around
here. Thought I heard voices. Don't they drive you a little
crazy?

Mayor Shorty
Couldn't say. Would I know it if they did?

Chief Joseph
My people say when you travel the high peaks you can

often hear the other side.

Chester

The other side? What other side?

Chief Joseph

The Spirit World of course.

Chester

Say, Mayor, this Virgil guy, does he have any bloodhounds?

Mayor Shorty

Yeh, sure. Just one. Ole Bluetooth. He's treed many a cougar in his day. But his A-team is Sultan, a twenty-five pound tiger tomcat and Sally, a ten pound long-haired dachshund. Between them from dawn to dusk they can rid a house or a barn Of rats, snakes, and any other varmints bigger than a bug. And they enjoy their work. Sultan once flushed a coyote out of a barn; that coyote didn't stop running til he hit the Pacific Ocean. Sultan and Garfield could swap stories.

Chester

Why can't we hire Bluetooth to track this monster?

Chief Joseph

Won't work. Your monster's a Wallamootka and Bluetooth has enough sense not to follow his trail because he knows he could never catch up with it. AND WOULDN'T WANT TO.

Tiffany

Say Chief, how do you know what this monster is? Why wouldn't a bloodhound follow its trail? Is it maybe a werewolf or something?

(Music plays. Dark Bach organ music)

(Mayor Shorty holds up one of the printouts.)

Mayor Shorty

That's what the Enquirer says it is. Says it's likely they'll
be vampires coming here also to check out the scene,
followed by those Christian vampire-hunters. And wolf-
watchers and wolf-haters. You know this might be an
opportunity for economic revival for this town. This Corona
business has made people crazier than usual. I better
call Stupifyin Jones and have her order more booze.

Chester

Who's Stupifyin Jones?

Mayor Shorty

Sally Jones, barmaid and proprietress of the Dogpatch
Saloon, the town's only bar and eatery. Richest person
in the county and biggest employer in the town.

Chester

Dogpatch? What kind of a name is that?

Mayor Shorty

It's a very American name, like apple pie and Pogo Possum.
Don't you guys ever read anything in your spare
time besides firearm manuals and terrorist profiles? I'll
bet you don't even know about Sadie Hawkins Day. The
one day every four years women are authorized to chase
men and pop the question. It's taken pretty serious around here.
You better watch your step on February 29th!

Chester

Why does she call herself Stupifyin Jones?

Mayor Shorty

She doesn't call herself that. We call her that. But never
to her face. That would be crude; you young guys have no
manners. After you seen her son if you don't know why
that's her nickname, visit the county's optometrist in

Winchester. Or Doc Seeley can give you some of that Viagra. (Music plays. Honky-tonk Piano / Dixieland / or Offenbach)

Chief Joseph
Your monster is not a werewolf, shapeshifter, or a regular wolf. It's a Wallamootka.

Chester
But how do you know it's a...whatever?

Chief Joseph
Because I read its tracks at the dump. Ole Bluetooth will take one sniff at the corpse hole, bay, and return to the truck. You won't get him to follow that trail for love, money, or even a T-bone steak. And your Wallamootka is a long-distance traveler. Probably won't check out the dump again for seven or eight days depending on how long his route is.

Chester
You mean this creature follows a regular route like a paper boy?

Chief Joseph
Say more like a cougar.

Mayor Shorty
Gentlemen, Chief Joseph's the best tracker in the state of Washington. Not only that, he's got a degree in biology from Harvard. If he says it's a whatever you better believe him. Long ago some crack-head held up the Dogpatch Saloon on Christmas Eve, got way confused in his getaway and went up Highway. 61. Chief Joseph tracked him for ten miles up Witch Mountain, after his car went off the highway in a blizzard. Brought back the body and the loot.

Chester
So, Chief, what's a Wallamootka?

Chief Joseph

In old Mandan, its name means "Great Small Warrior Who Travels Alone." You white people are sloppy with names, they mean nothing. Indians try to give each other names that tell you something about the people or animals to which they refer. The Mootka are small but mighty and fierce warriors like the wolf people and bear people. As you can see by my headband my totem clan is wolf. The Mootka clan has always been tiny. Virtually no white man and few Indians have ever seen them. But they, unlike people, run free and alone. Going where they will among the valleys, meadows, rivers, tundra, and snowy peaks; running up frozen waterfalls like your crazy mountain climbers with crampons and ice axes. Nothing stops them. They don't count cost. Only your Mountain Men once lived like the Mootka. Don't you yet know what I'm talking about? Your scientists label them "Gulo, Gulo" a somewhat ridiculous name as we know now. Gulo means glutton in Latin. Anyone lives in snow country is always hungry.

Chester

Is that like a Yeti or Sasquatch?

Chief Joseph

No, it's a...

(HONK! HONK!)

(Mabel Stokely runs in the door)

Mabel

The Press is here! The Press is here! There's even a TV crew. They're interviewing Gary and Bowser right now.

(Pandemonium ensues. They all exit Mayor's office.)

CHORUS

Listen to the music of the night.

(Sirens blare, car horns honk, coyotes wail)

ACT 1 SCENE 4

(In front of the Bakery/General Store, a rustic western wood-frame structure with two plastic chairs bracketing the entrance. Present are Gary, Bowser and Mayor Shorty)

(CNN camera crew enters)

                    CNN Talking Head Milt Hartley
(speaking to Mayor Shorty)
Sir, do you have any novel Corona around here?

                    Mayor Shorty
If you're looking for that virus, we don't have any. Doc knows every-body in town and can vouch for that. You need to go over to Kirkland or Seattle. Maybe they still have some. We don't have any of the other three Corona viruses that annoy humans either. Nor Hantavirus.

                    CNN Talking Head Milt Hartley
Who saw this supposed monster?

                    Mayor Shorty
(pointing to Gary and Bowser)
Talk to these two.

                    CNN Talking Head Milt Hartley
Say son, you live here?

                    Gary
Gary Gardiano, Town Dumpmaster.

                              CNN
You believe in this monster, Gary?

                              Gary
I believe in what I saw. I'm the one that called Chief Fenton.

                              Bowser
WOOF! WOOF!

                              CNN
What's your dog saying?

                              Gary
Hell if I know. Ask him yourself.

                              CNN
So what did this so-called monster look like?

                              Gary
Had blue-green sort of luminous eyes. It was black and growled as loud as a grizzly when I disturbed its dinner with my flashlight and it disappeared in a wink.

                              CNN
So what do you think it was?

                              Gary
Don't know. Maybe something came over from Glacier Park. Ask our town biologist, Chief Joseph.

                              CNN
The guy you phoned?

                              Gary
No, that was Chief Fenton.

                              CNN
You trying to pull my leg, son?

Gary

Not after all the leg pulling I saw last night. Of course Chief
Fenton first thought it might be Hillary.

CNN

(Looks nervously over his shoulder at his cameraman)
What?

Gary (deadpan)

That's Prospector Mike's burro. She disappears every year about
this time. Chief Joseph says she has a boyfriend on the mountain.
A Bighorn or Billy.

CNN(still wary)

A billy?

Gary

Yep! That's a male mountain goat. This is one of the few places in
America you can see one.

CNN

Why does he call his burro 'Hillary?'

Gary (pointing)

Why don't you ask him yourself, he's over there.

CNN (addressing Prospector Mike)

How are you today, sir?

Mike

Still above ground, thank you.

CNN

Why did you name your burro Hillary?

Mike (with tears in his eyes)

After an old girlfriend of mine who ran off and married a...

                         CNN
A lawyer?

                         Mike
Nah. She did better than that. A televangelist!

                         CNN
And you sir, what political party are you affiliated with?

                         Mike
Last time I was affiliated I was a Wobbly.

                         CNN
A Wobbly?

                         Mike
Yes sir. I used to be a real pistol when I was younger.

(Mayor Shorty enters and whispers to Gary)

                    Mayor Shorty (whispering)
Stall 'em Gary. Rattle off some statistics or something.
You're good at those.

                         Gary
The mayor says I should tell you something about our town. We
have 223 people who live here. Every house has a rainwater basin.
Our drinking water comes from Lake Snowtop where we have
a modern all-weather communal water pump. Better than Fuji
Water. The air is pure, 'cept during a chili cook-off or pig races.
Our unemployment rate is 42%. The county unemployment rate
is 37.37% as measured by banker P. Stevens of Winchester last
Labor Day.

                         CNN
You don't use Federal Census data?

                         Gary
Out of date! That's trash. Priscilla Stevens, banker, with the help

of her Saturday afternoon tea group knows the employment status of every person in Winchester County. Her 37.37 is a real world number unlike government rates based on 'cock-a-doodle-do I don't see you' computer models that under report the real rate by half. The Feds don't wanna count the 'invisible people' as she calls them, those that have run out of unemployment benefits and can't be wasting gas going down to the unemployment office to be told there's nothing on offer.

CNN

What's the Democratic/Republican ratio in this county?

Gary

Exactly 50/50.

CNN

What you mean exactly?

Gary

There's one Teddy Roosevelt Republican and one Harry Truman Democrat! The rest are Independents.

CNN

So ladies and gentlemen, that's how it is this afternoon in Snowtop, Washington. Where last night a green-eyed ghoul feasted on a human corpse in the town dump. Can anyone be safe with a creature like that on the loose?

(Milt, Gary, Prospector Mike, and Bowser exit. Mabel and Tiffany enter and sit down in the plastic chairs.)

(Mabel waves to Gary who is offstage.)

Mabel

Well done, Gary!

(Tiffany looks offstage in a different direction.)

Tiffany

Wow, Mabel. Who's that huge hunk of a man wearing
a sheepskin vest? I'm getting warm and tingly all over.

Mabel

Cool down, young lady. That's Pedro Larranaga, our
Basque sheepherder. Tell you about him later. Meanwhile
what do you think of Gary?

Tiffany

Your Dumpmaster? Impressive presence for a young man. I
like the way he kept to facts and let Hartley do the hyperbole.
Wish all witnesses were that good. Oh, who was that elderly
Japanese man who saw us just now and suddenly turned tail.

Mabel

Saw you, Tiff, and knew you were with the FBI. Mr. Yamasaki
is a careful and cautious man. He grows fruit, vegetables and
flowers locally and has no peer in the garden arts. My store sells
everything he raises. Came here in January 1942, with his family
when he was ten.

Tiffany

I remember. To escape Manzanar and those other places.

Mabel

Right. Other branches of the Yamasaki clan are also famous
in the garden arts in the gold rush area of the Sierra foothills
above Sacramento.

Tiffany

So when did this hunk Pedro get here? I speak a little Spanish.
Can't women fantasize? Why should men have all the fun?
He doesn't look like he needs to be shy or cautious.

Mabel

You might be surprised. Even though Pedro was born
here thirty years ago, and speaks indifferent English

and Spanish, his Basque is excellent and he's real old-fashioned. However, if you could speak to him in Basque, you would have a date in five minutes. Like a traditional country Basque he tosses boulders and logs around in those crazy games of theirs. Usually has to go down to Elko for those where the Star Hotel can fix you up with a Basque meal your stomach won't forget for two days. If you check the historical records for the port of Valparaiso, Chile, for January 1849, under passengers departing for California with Basque surnames, you will find Pedro T. Larranaga made passage on the Brigantine Felix Araucano. That was Pedro's great-grandfather who arrived at Snowtop in 1854.

Tiffany

Wow, he sounds really interesting. If Pedro were Chief of Police I doubt you would have much crime.

Mabel

Maybe not. Yet Phil's got common sense, knows when to talk and when to shoot. Knows better than to set up speed traps in a town bent on tourism. You notice how dark he is; his great, great grandfather was one of those Buffalo Soldiers. But, in a way we do use Pedro in law enforcement. He's part of our town civil defense plan. If there's a town emergency like a fire or a motorcycle gang shows up at Dogpatch, someone clangs the bell outside of Shorty's office three times.

Tiffany

What happens at Dogpatch?

Mabel

Sally doesn't discriminate against any customer, regardless of sartorial or sexual preference-if they behave themselves. The bell is just to call Pedro in to do emergency bouncer duty and to alert his replacement, like Gary or Carlos, to do sheep duty. We take care of each other here and try to prevent trouble before it happens.

Tiffany
I can see that you do. Oops, there's my boss waving at me.
Got to go.

(Tiffany exits and Mayor Shorty enters)

Mayor Shorty
Mabel, more bad news already. Just got a call from the
Rodeo Board pulling our town's August 10th date. Said
we've become too controversial-and we don't have a
decent motel or even a gas station. I've a message to
call the State Fair Committee, probably they'll tell me
having a monster come visit, is not good modeling for
4H or Junior Achievement programs! And some
minister from a church in Hillsboro informed me our
monster was the devil and the world will end August 2nd.
And the Cowboy Poetry Contest for Labor Day was
cancelled too.

Mabel
I'm sure glad you're mayor this year, Shorty, and not me.

Mayor Shorty
Yeah. When I drew the short straw at our New Year's Eve party
I looked at the four of you and got the eeriest feeling, a kind of
premonition that things would go bad for me this time. I even
tried to convince Mr. Yamasaki to run for mayor in my place!

(Mayor Shorty exits and Tiffany enters)

Mabel
So what chore did your boss have for you?

Tiffany
To show Milt Hartley the corpse. Milt fears being made a
fool of and wanted to confirm Gary's statements that the
corpse had been munched on.

Mabel

Did he get his confirmation?

Tiffany

Sure did. And upchucked on your grass afterwards.

Mabel

Don't worry about it. I see Bluetooth has already smelled
it and is headed that way. He's getting on in years and isn't
finicky about predigested meals. Bowser wouldn't touch
it; the insolence of youth.

(Tiffany looks offstage)

Tiffany

My goodness! Who was that handsome cowboy with the
silver spurs and bridle? Where are you hiding these guys?

Mabel

Carlos Chama, Chief Joseph's head wrangler. Also helps
Pedro with the sheep sometimes. Especially if there's a
cougar, wolf or bear around. The Chief also uses fladry
and Great Pyrenees sheep dogs.

Tiffany

A cowboy helping run sheep? That's a new one. Hope
he carries his green card around these days. Immigration
is tightening up our northern border, we've been told.
You've heard of ICE?

Mabel

Carlos isn't Mexican; his family came to Santa Fe with
Juan de Oñate in 1595 from Spain. One of his great-
grandfathers was fighting the Chiricahua Apache in 1776
at the siege of Santa Cruz de Terrenate. He could well ask
us for our green cards. But good Spanish manners would
prevent it.

Tiffany
So how long has Carlos known Pedro?

Mabel
They grew up together. Carlos even knows some Basque.
Carlos and Pedro sometimes sing to the cows and sheep in
Basque—and it puts them to sleep really fast. We once
had a sheep singing contest, but the judges fell asleep too!

Tiffany
I see. Your town is a regular melting pot of cultures. Say
Mabel, how can you be Post-mistress, Justice of the Peace,
and town merchant?

Mabel
In tiny towns or rural areas this sort of thing is just necessary.
To live in the country you have to be a generalist. Need to
know about lots of things. Like how to fix your septic tank or
field, or your wood burning stove or do a garden. You city
folks are specialists. Our local doc is a cardiologist turned GP.
Got tired of the cardio patient turnover (and turnunder)
in Seattle.

Tiffany
Oops. Chester again. Got to go.

(Tiffany exits)

(The bell clangs loudly three times)

Mabel
Oh my! What a day! What's next? Hope it's not gremlins
again!

END OF ACT ONE

ACT 2, SCENE 1

(The Dogpatch Restaurant, an old-fashioned diner with western/
country decor.)

(Present are Mayor Shorty, Chief Joseph, Mabel Stokely, Chief Fenton,
and FBI agents Chester and Tiffany, and DEA agent Walter)

Mayor Shorty
Mornin' ladies and gents. Hope you all slept well over at
the Hotel Snowtop.

Chester
So, so. Fairly comfortable old beds but I heard a lot of skittering
around. But no street traffic noise even with all those media
people in town. Nice lobby and lounge. Neat fireplace! And I
like your mounted jackelope head. Never seen one. Must be an
endangered species.

Mayor Shorty (smiling)
Could be! I imagine Sultan and Sally will be finishing off the
cleanup job they started yesterday. You won't hear any more
skittering noise.

Chester
We sure looked dumb on CNN trying to get Bluetooth to
follow that monster's trail, particularly when we dangled
a T-bone steak in front of him. He just snuffled, turned his
soulful eyes on his tempter and sat back down again.

Chief Joseph
Bluetooth is a smart dog and old-fashioned like the people here.

Won't take your pay if they haven't done the job. And he knew taking the steak meant taking on the job. Country dogs are smarter than your city pampered pooch, they have to use their wits.

Tiffany
Never ever seen a dog turn down a steak before!

Mayor Shorty
Cheer up guys. CNN loved that sequence. They're more into entertainment than news anyway. And they really enjoyed the night feast sequence with your super-duper night camera showing the coyotes and mice feeding on the cow carcasses you left for the monster. I know you use it for drug lords and terrorists but if we had one of those, we might go into eco-tourism.

Chester
I like your old-fashioned town, no one wears masks.

Mabel
Why should they; who wants to look like a duck? If we get too many tourists I might have to stock masks at the store. Que sera sera! People in this valley are too busy just staying alive. Why worry over something over which you have little control?

(At Director's option, Chorus – offstage – sings the 4 bars of Doris Day's hit song, "Que Sera, Sera")

Chief Joseph
You know, Mayor, that high bare ridge above town is an animal highway. I've seen deer tracks, cougar, wolf and even an occasional bear print. How good is that tele-camera?

Tiffany
Five hundred power with good clarity and resolution by day or night. During a full moon it's spooky. It's like looking at living ghosts.

Mayor Shorty
So what's on your agenda for today, guys?

Chester
We're leavin'. There's nothing more for us here, we're thinking.

Mayor Shorty
You're joking!

Chester
The FBI has no sense of humor that we are aware of.

Walter
I can confirm that. I was canned from the bureau for "excess jocularity." Mostly they didn't like my terrorist jokes. You know, like… "Why did the terrorist cross the road?" Stuff like that. "How many terrorists does it take to stuff a letter bomb?"

Chief Joseph
Don't you want to find out about the red dust where Mr. Guerrero spent his first burial? Could be it was that Navajo Sandstone outcropping on Witch Mountain. Likely hideout for a drug gang. There's a couple of old caves there and even an old mine that's been padlocked. Good place to land a copter nearby.

(Sally Jones enters. The out-of-town gents wear a stupefied leer.)

Sally
How's your breakfasts, gentlemen? And yours Miz Gates? I'm your hostess, Sally Jones. How are you this morning, Mabel?

Mabel
Just fine thanks Sally. Good to see you getting so much business, dearie.

Sally
Thanks sweetie. Noticed your bakery was doing a land office business in donuts this morning.

Mabel

You're right. Herbert's working his tail off.

Sally

Let me know, gentlemen, and you Miz Gates, if there's anything you need and I hope to see you again.

(Sally exits)

Chester

That was Stupifyin Jones wasn't it?

(Chorus: Wolf whistles, "Wows" and clapping fill the dining room)

Mayor Shorty

Now gents, take notice there's ladies present.

Mabel

It's all right, Mayor. We ladies use that nickname too. Discretely of course.

Chester

You know, guys, we need to maybe check out this here place the Chief mentioned. This Witch Mountain. Maybe we can even stay another night and sew things up.

(All the Federales nod their heads emphatically and clap.)

Mayor Shorty

A nice, diplomatic approach, son, they should transfer you to the higher levels at the State Department.

Walter

Won't happen. They don't want diplomats up at that altitude; they want people who test high on the old schoolmarm scold index.

Chester
Let's go guys. On to Witch Mountain. Banzai!

(All exit diner)

ACT 2, SCENE 2

(In front of the Shack at the Dump)

(Present are Gary, Bowser, Mayor Shorty, Chief Joseph, Mabel Stokely, Charley Cruikshank, and Sally Jones; all are seated on folding chairs or stools.)

Sally
Mayor, introduce me to these two young gentleman. Never formally met them before. Seen them around of course.

Mayor Shorty
Sally, this is Gary Gardiano, our Dumpmaster. And this is Bowser, our Junkyard Dog.

Gary
Pleased to meet you, Miz Jones.

Sally
Gary, just call me Sally, please.

Bowser
WOW! WOW! WOW!

Sally
Why thank you, Bowser. You're a very handsome devil yourself.

Mayor Shorty

Sally is Director of Economic Development for the town as you all know. I wanted her here for this think session. We're trying to figure out why Mr. G was ignominiously planted in our dump. The Feds don't think it's important. They made a great publicity coup yesterday by finding the drug gang's hideout. Thanks to Chief Joseph who took them right there. But they did their own shooting when they got there. Turns out Mohammed was sort of a folk hero. He held off the rival gang single-handedly for all of three minutes.

Charley

The rival gang gave him a proper red dust burial and when Mohammed's gang came back there was another merry shootout. Then, they had a truce during which the rival gang, the Loco Mokos, agreed to return Mohammed's corpse. It's the Loco Mokos the Feds had a shootout with. Mohammed's gang agreed to leave off their attack so they could properly bury their chief on their way south.

Mabel

Take a look at these photos of the crime scene they've loaned us.

(Photos passed around)

Charley

Maybe the guys that buried him made a mistake. This cemetery annex is right behind this section of the dump. And there's no fence between.

Sally

What's this white thing on the ground in this photo? It's right next to the hole he was in.

(Hands photo to Gary)

Gary

Jumpin' Jehosaphat! I know what happened. Charley is right.

Mayor Shorty

What is it Gary?

Gary

It's one of those white crosses we use to mark temporary graves in the cemetery. Our backhoe driver Willis is a bit weird. When he digs us a 36-foot trench for the next load of garbage he places white crosses every 6 feet of the trench afterwards. It's his joke. He calls it giving the garbage a proper Christian burial. Mr. Guerrero was buried in the last six foot section of this trench. When those guys arrived it was dark and they would have seen a pre-dug grave with a white cross on it.

Sally

Thinking they were in the cemetery in holy ground.

Gary

Exactly!

Mayor Shorty

Bravo Team! There's no longer a mystery. He was buried here on purpose, but by accident, by his friends.

Gary

Who stiffed us for the $100 burying fee?

Mabel

But they were in a hurry. City people always are. Government and the media have colluded to change their way of thinking. They no longer have a problem to solve, invariably it's a 'crisis.' One of the reasons Americans are such short-term thinkers.

(Walter enters in a rush)

Walter

Bad news coming people! Thought I would give you a heads-up so you could figure out what to do. If anything. They're going to leave what's left of Mohammed's corpse.

Gary

That's not a problem. We'll bury it properly. We're a legal cemetery and are used to Potters Field burials. We even have 'Other Species' authorization. We're a pet cemetery sanctioned by the SPCA. The Highway Patrol brings us lots of bodies and parts of bodies—mostly from Highway 61—who died of cellularitis. They happily pay our hundred dollar burial fee to get shed of these corpses.

Walter

What's cellularitis?

Gary

Trying to answer your cellular telephone while going round the mountain curves of Highway 61.

Walter

Interesting. You guys are trendsetters; you've put a neat name to a national affliction. Almost forgot. You don't understand the bad news yet. Homeland Security won't pay a burial fee for Mohammed because they think he's Al Qaeda. I overheard the conversation they had on speakerphone with the #2 Man, General Hardpence. Their exact instructions are to dump Mohammed out in the open desert scrub somewhere where the buzzards and dogs can get at him, refuse to pay any fees to bury him, and to recycle his body bag.

Phil

Recycle his body bag? Yuck! How are they gonna do that? That must violate some Washington State health statutes or something. Like reusing needles. And if they toss that body bag in the bushes, I could get them for littering, and that's a twenty-five dollar city fine.

Charley

You're forgetting that dumping Mohammed's corpse on the desert is also littering of the grossest kind. However, I suggest holding back that card for a while until we see if the Feds are going to play hardball. No use humiliating anyone just for the hell of it.

Walter
You people have a canny consiglieri here. I like this man.

Chief Joseph
How do they even know this Mohammed is Al Qaeda? His bride
might have been on the outs with her cousin. And Mohammed's
only related by marriage.

Gary
We can't let them do this. They're way beyond cheap, they're
mean. Why, we don't even leave horse thieves and cattle rustlers
to the coyotes and buzzards. Even an outlaw or drifter, or a
mortgage broker, banker, or politician deserves a decent burial.
It's one of those unwritten laws of the West. This General
Hardpence reminds me of that old Greek guy in one of those
scary old plays. His name was Creep-On or Odeon or something.
This babe wanted to bury her brother but this tyrant dude…

Mayor Shorty
Creon.

Gary
Right! Creon said anyone who buries that corpse would be stoned
to death. Because the brother had been exiled and joined an
opposition party in another island and came back fighting with
them. And lost. The gods of the Greeks said every man deserved a
proper burial and to leave the corpse to jackals and buzzards was
a sacrilege.

Mayor Shorty
That's right, Gary. In Sophocles' own words, this burying was part
of "The immortal unrecorded laws of God."

Gary
Those Greek guys thought a man's ghost would wander around
unhappy and maybe even bother people if it wasn't buried proper.

Sally

And so Antigone, preferring death with honor to life with dishonor buried her brother and was done in by Creon. A woman's libber that lived two thousand five hundred years ago. Say Mr. DEA man, why are you helping us?

Walter

Course you already know I've got some of the Celtic craziness in me—but I like you people. You're old-fashioned and I don't care if that's out of style. And you're decent and have true grit. Most people these days are on Planet Selfish especially those plutocrats on Wall Street. And the oligarchs inside the Beltway. You're like Main Street America used to be. And God save us from all those do-gooding billionaires!

Sally

You're welcome at the Dogpatch Saloon any time partner. On the house!

Walter

Thanks!

Charley

Thanks for your help, Walt.

Walter

Whoa! Here comes weird Willis bringing you the papers on all this. They're using him as a messenger and general dogs-body.

Bowser

BOW WOW! BOW WOW!

Walter

Oh I'm sorry, Bowser. That was certainly an insensitive canine slur I used. By the way, they plan to toss Mohammed's corpse off that old dirt spur road round the first curve up Highway 61. They're probably doing it now.

Sally
They going to keep their seven PM dinner reservation?

Walter
Oh sure. We'll all be there but we're driving on to Spokane
afterwards where they have us billeted at the local Motel eight
and a half. By the way, who owns that mine where we had our
OK Corral shootout with the Loco Mokos? In all the brouhaha
there was an explosion and a whole new chamber got revealed.
Might make the mine profitable now. My old man was a mining
engineer in Nevada City. His dad did some gold panning around
Alder Gulch, Montana, I think.

Sally
That mine is mine, Walter, pardon the pun. Belonged to my
granddad and made possible the building of the Snowtop Hotel.
If you have any free time before dinner, see me.

Walter
How's six o'clock?

Sally
Fine!

Chief Joseph
I'll mosey on out there and see if I can retrieve Mr. Guerrero's
remains.

Gary
I just thought of something. We have another ally; the Pope!
Mohammed was wearing a gold crucifix and he's Columbian.
Despite his first names I'd lay odds he was a Catholic! Say
Mabel, speaking officially as Dumpmaster, can you add me on
an emergency basis to your four P.M. Small Claims Court open
hearing today. I'm going to make a claim against the Feds for
Mohammed's burying fee.

Mabel
You're on the schedule, Dumpmaster. Remember, as soon as you get the paper from Willis, make a proper written response and claim, and have him deliver it Pronto Tonto.

Sally
Chief Joseph and I want to meet with him in about an hour regarding some economic development issues. Is that alright, Gary? At Dogpatch in the back room.

Gary
You bet Miz...uh Sally.

ACT 2, SCENE 3

(Supply room of the Dogpatch Restaurant's kitchen, 3:00 P.M.)

(Present are Sally, Gary, Bowser, Margo, and Charley. All seated at a supply table on which is perched a cardboard casket.)

(Chief Joseph enters carrying a heavy sack.)

Bowser
BOW WOW GLUCK!

Sally
Bowser, you're right. We better get the corpse sealed up in the box right away.

(Chief Joseph deposits sack in the casket and they start to seal it up.)

Bowser
BOW WOW YUCK!

Gary

Okay, dog, cool it. We're getting the job done.

(In walks Chief Fenton with a smaller sack.)

Chief Fenton

I found it! I've got the evidence. Those damn Federal litterers didn't even try to bury the body bag. Everybody thinks the desert is an open trash can.

Margo

Gee Chief, that stinks. Put another garbage bag over it. He don't smell very kosher!

Gary

You're right Margo, Bowser sniffed it even before Phil walked in the door. Thing is, every now and then it seems like Bowser is talking English.

Sally

Anybody recover the gold crucifix?

(All shake their heads in a 'No.')

Sally (continues)

Phil, maybe you better talk to those Feds now and find out what happened to it. We can add your request for a littering fine to other stuff we're requesting of the judge.

Phil

Good idea, Sally. Let me go talk to those guys before they check out.

(Phil exits)

Chief Joseph

Charley, can we ask the judge to let us keep that telescope-camera as security for their refusal to pay the burial fee?

Charley

I'll give you a qualified 'yes.' But your best chance is to put together an economic development plan right here and now. Some tourism gig. And ask the judge to allow you to use this equipment for such specific purposes. Otherwise, you'll have to lock it up and that wouldn't get us anyplace.

Gary

Tourism? Like to show the monster feeding on the cow carcasses at night? That would be cool! Or stargazing? Or looking for wolves? Why should Yellowstone get all the wolf-watching business?

Margo

And to eyeball that animal highway during the day. Might even make some trails up to it. Vacationers that hike eat a lot more donuts. And do more hotel stays and restaurant meals.

Sally

And look at the bird life on Lake Snowtop which we could rename the Doc Seeley Bird Sanctuary, since he owns most of the property here anyway. And he knows dozens of those Audubon bird people nationally.

(Phil runs in the door holding the crucifix.)

Phil

Got it! They gave it to me before I even asked.

Sally

Good work Chief!

Chief Joseph

Good work fellow Chief.

Gary

I never knew Chief Joseph had a sense of humor. Say, Chief, what is a Wallamootka?

(A suffocating silence envelops the room.)

Chief Joseph
I can see by your expressions that only two of you know, besides
Bluetooth.

Bowser
WOOF! WOOF!

Chief Joseph
Sorry Bowser. You're wrong. But good guess. What you smelled
and saw that night was a wolverine. One of the rarest and most
amazing animals on the planet. These little critters have been
known to back down grizzly bears. Your real hard-core nature nut
is going to come a long way to see one of these. On the WAITING
LIST (only 250 ahead of them) for listing as an endangered
species.

Charley
No kidding?

Chief Joseph
You bet! Let me lend you my copy of "The Wolverine Way" by
Douglas Chadwick. That guy admires them so much he wishes
he could be one. Surely it must be his totem. Wallamootka!
The Wolf Clan salutes you!

Charley
Listing didn't help the wolf much. Their state residency card now
determines how—and how soon—they die after putting one paw
over a national park boundary line.

Sally
Margo, you look unhappy.

Margo
I was looking forward to doing G and G tourism.

Gary

What's that?

Margo

Ghosts and ghouls. That's the new thing these days.

Charley

Maybe we can play that card too. One of those reporters last time told me he was checking out the rumor that OUR Chief Joseph was THE Chief Joseph. I had to admit our Joseph knows a lot about his great-great grandfather. He's an amateur historian of the period. This reporter named Kojak didn't pay attention when I said Joseph and I grew up together and he was like an uncle to me. The guy thinks our Chief is a vampire and the old Joseph. The Wolf Clan stuff is a smokescreen. He says Pedro Larranaga our Basque sheepherder is our werewolf because he's shaggy, strong, and lives at the edge of town, even though I told him Chief Joseph's Great Pyrenees dogs love him.

Margo

They only hear what they want to hear.

Sally

Like the Feds. And voters. Well, without being dishonest, we can make it work for us. I take it we're all agreed?

(All stand up and raise their right hands in clenched fist salute.)

ALL (shouting)

Eco-tourism forever!

(All exit)

CHORUS (shout first line)

WALLAMOOTKA PLEASE RETURN!
May the forest be with us.
Smokey Bear watch over us.
Hug a tree. Peace be to thee.

May the Wolf Spirits of the Nootka guide our howls.

(Chorus howls like wolves)

ACT 2, SCENE 4

(Supply room of the Dogpatch Restaurant's kitchen, 6:00 P.M.)

(Present are Sally and Walter)

Sally
Grandpa's mining chemicals and logbook are over there.

Walter
Can I use them? I know what I'm doing. I've got an ore sample
From your new chamber in my hanky.

Sally
Go ahead, I trust you. I always know when men are feeding me a
line.

Walter
Useful skill for a gorgeous gal like yourself.

Sally
It has come in handy. Specially back east in that Ivy League
college my dad sent me to. It was this same gold mine that did it
too. I was born and raised rich but now the money's almost gone
and the town still thinks I'm in clover because they're so poor. But
I love the people here. And I think they love me too.

(Walter mixes chemicals into the ore samples at the worktable)

Walter

Sally, I can tell they do. And young lady, you have some high
grade gold ore here. If you sold to one of those mega-corp mining
outfits you could be the new Molly Brown.

Sally

Thanks Walt, that's what I was afraid of. I've done young Molly
but I don't want to be Molly B. again. Nor do I want to be any
rich man's trophy wife. Walt, Witch Creek drains down into Lake
Snowtop. You know what would happen to the town of Snowtop
if a modern gold mine was put in up there. It would trash the
water supply first, then the town itself, in no time at all.

Walter

You're an amazing woman, Sally. Wish I were twenty-five years
younger.

Sally

Walt, my dumb heart is set on another, but he hasn't all together
grown up yet. We were kids together but his dad was a coal miner
and he himself took seven years to earn his law degree in night
school. Still poor as a church mouse, as if I care. He's a fine
teacher. Been honored with national awards and runs one of the
few single-room schools left in America. Neither he nor his pupils
wear masks. And he doesn't do any of that distance learning.

Walter

Too bad for the two of you. But you know, people can change
overnight sometimes.

Sally

Granddad said his mine was run pretty clean. He never did
placer. Do the stamp mill and smelter still look good in there?

Walter

As far as I can tell. At today's insane gold prices you should be
able to make a go of it small-scale. An upfront cash reserve would
be best business practice. It would be labor intensive and you

would have to pay out a lot of money in wages before you show any return.

Sally

But that's just what I want. To give my fellow townsmen some jobs. It's clear the government has forgotten us after taking care of the fat cats first.

Walter

I see your point. Maybe de-industrialization is the best answer to perennial systemic unemployment.

Sally

Why don't they send rural areas some stimulus money in the form of firebreak building and tree thinning jobs? The national parks and forests around here could use it—before the next firestorms. And those jobs can't be done by machines.

Walter

Good point! And big cities have machines that maybe should be retired, like those so-called street cleaning behemoths that just stir the dust around with their huge brushes and push chunky trash into drain outlets, stopping them up. Unemployed people with pushcarts would give us cleaner cities. Our big cities also seem to harbor—or breed—hysterics, histrionics, and hypochondriacs too. But those types don't survive out here, I'm thinking.

Sally

As for cash reserve, don't have that kind of green. We don't trust banks anymore either. Except for Winchester Savings. And Priscilla couldn't handle that; she's barely surviving now. People here are desperate enough to work for free if it were a cooperative operation.

Walter

What can you lose but your sweat?

Sally

I'll read over granddad's notes. I did take chemistry. If you can recommend a book or monograph on the subject…

Walter

I'll send it to you. Maybe a couple months from now I can talk my boss into sending me here to make sure the druggies haven't re-infested your mine. I better head back now, it's dinner time.

Sally

I'll walk you there, Walt. And tell people I'm reopening Grandpa's mine based on what you saw in there. After your guys have gone, I'll tell everybody you're our mining consultant as well.

Walter

Nice idea, Sally. You're a brick!

Sally

And built like a brick shithouse the boys used to say when they thought I couldn't hear them.

Walter

In regard to you, both things are true.

Sally

You're a devil of a flirt, Walter.

Walter

Oh shoot! My cover's been blown!

(A loud knock is heard at the door)

Sally

Come in. We were just leaving.

(Margo and Mabel enter)

Margo

Sally, hope you don't mind, we're bringing Carlos in here for an inside audition.

Sally

An audition?

Margo

We've listened to him and Pedro sing and play Spanish music at their campsite. Carlos recites long passages of an old epic poem in Spanish. They're both very entertaining, but Pedro's a little stage-shy. We got to thinking that if we're to attract tourists here, we've got to have some nighttime entertainment over at the hotel and at your place. Although their singing puts the sheep to sleep, we're hoping it will have an opposite effect on people.

Mabel

Actually, it was Tiffany's idea. She's in the barn now with Carlos as he's warming up his guitar and vocal cords. Meantime he's teaching her Basque and Spanish simultaneously. That girl has a gift for languages. Should have worked for the State Department.

Sally

Sounds like a good contingency plan to me, but remember Carlos has other duties.

Margo

We thought about that too. If we get lots of tourists we might try a "Visiting Shepherd" program, giving them the overnight experience of watching Chief Joseph's sheep.

Sally

You think tourists will pay to watch someone's sheep?

Margo

Never know til you try. There's all those reality TV shows out there. Disney couldn't do it but I bet we could. We have discussed this briefly with Chief Joseph.

Sally

And what did he say?

Margo

Says the idea is totally crazy, and therefore might possibly work.

Sally

Why not try it? Sail on!

Walter

I think so too. You have to look at all the cards you have and play the best. Chief Joseph's people were sure smart coming here. I've seen the Nez Perce reservation in Lapwai, Idaho. People should always be on the scout for opportunity.

Mabel

You sound like a modern Dale Carnegie.

Walter

Wanna be my literary agent?

Mabel

I've had worse offers.

Sally

Walt and I were just leaving. Carry on ladies.

(All exit together)

END OF ACT TWO

ACT 3, SCENE 1

(Dogpatch Restaurant)

(Present are Sally, Charley, Phil, Mayor Shorty, and Mabel)

(Gary comes running in with Bowser)

Bowser
WOOFVEEN! WOOFVEEN!

Gary
What Bowser is trying to say is the wolverine is back. He's
busy chomping away on those cow bones and selected pieces of
garbage I laid out. Come see! It's super cool. I've got the
camera on automatic. Run!

Charley
The chief was right. This is the eighth day since Wallamootka's
debut. Not only that, he's arrived on Earth Day. That's got to be
a positive portent. Let's go see it. Maybe Gary got something
CNN would like. And we'll call the Winchester Weekly tomorrow
morning. Things are looking up again.

(All exit)

CHORUS
Here comes the Media Money Machine.
Make famous, make you rich.
Here come de green!
Here come de green!
Here come de wolverine!

ACT 3, SCENE 2

(Dogpatch Restaurant, 3:00 P.M., July 5)

(Mabel and Sally are having tea together at a small table)

Mabel
So how's business at Dogpatch, Sweetie?

Sally
I'm swamped, Mabel. Hired everybody in town that doesn't
have the dropsies. If we didn't catch those scamps trying to
steal the telescope yesterday, I'd be laying these people off.
How clever to use Fourth of July when we have a town fiesta
as cover for their caper. We owe Pedro.

Mabel
We sure do!

Sally
Funny thing, he said not to worry, the gods of the forest had
already repaid him.

Mabel
I wonder. Pedro was one of those old pagan Basques, I think.
Well, let's get to business. Eco-tourism has filled the hotel
and nearly swamped your restaurant and my store. Your idea of
telling people that Snowtop is still a corona-free zone may have
doubled our reservations.

Sally
Can't last. Come September first reservations dry up. We need
to get the Witch Mountain mine up and running. By the way,
some Swiss yodeling group wants to rent the mine for a day

because they heard the echoes around there are spectacular.

Mabel

Let's look at the bright present for a change and let the future
worry about itself.

Sally

According to Margo's schedule sheet, on Wednesday it's Boy
Scout Troop 114 from Spokane. They're hiking up to the plateau
for a nature walk. On Thursday, it's Seattle Rotary. They've
booked helicopter nature tours. On Friday, we have the Hillsboro
Christian Apocalypse Center. They've reserved prime telescope
time two nights running. Don't want to miss Wallamootka. They
think he's the devil incarnate. I guess they're fascinated, like
people staring into a campfire.

Mabel

And losing their night vision.

Sally

Saturday night we've got the Seattle Gay/Lesbian Alliance.
They've booked the Carlos and Pedro show solid.

Mabel

Really? Maybe they think Carlos and Pedro are the
reincarnation of Bud and Travis.

Sally

The Winchester Weekly gave them a good review.
And one of the Seattle critics called them "Refreshing."

(Margo runs in)

Margo

News! There's a strange guy just checked in. He has an
enclosed mobile medical gurney but I gotta look inside
of it when the armed attendant went to pee. It's a coffin!

Sally

I hope you checked his credit card.

Margo

Solid gold, Triple AAA.

Mabel

Do we have a vacationing vampire? Or just someone who
thinks he is?

Margo

Didn't peek in the coffin but my goosebumps tell me he's
the real McCoy. I'm wearing a silver crucifix.

Mabel

But you're Jewish, Margo!

Margo

When dealing with the supernatural I think you gotta
hedge your bets.

Mabel

But listen sweetie, I overheard him ask Chief Joseph to guide him
to Hidden Valley to the site of the '01 rodent Bubonic Plague
outbreak.

Margo

Really? Do you think he doesn't know there's places like that all
over
the Wild West?

Mabel

He's just a vampire wannabe weirdo. Joe laughed and told him he
wouldn't take his own mother-in-law there to meet Pasturella
Pestis!

(Mabel answers her cell phone, Margo walks out)

Mabel (speaking to Sally)
Herb says he just had six hulks come asking for those new
all year aerial wolf hunting permits the State of Washington
just authorized. He told them nearest permit station was in
Winchester. They bought local topos too. They were
carrying a rack of fancy rifles in their pickup.

(Margo runs back in)

Margo
A helicopter just landed. Has "Winchester Rentals" on the side.

Mabel
You don't suppose...

Sally
I do. Get Shorty and Phil in here, and Charley and Chief Joseph
if they're around town. Soonest. WE need a city council quorum.
Wolf watching is half our current tourism business and if one of
those
trigger-happy city slickers shoots Wallamootka, we'll be out of the
tourism business.

(All exit except Sally, who answers her cellphone)

Sally
Gary, what's happening?

Gary (offstage)
Help me please. I'm here at my post at the telescope. Just
Bowser and me. Senora Guerrero and Senorita Ines
Suarez Guerrero are here!

Sally
REALLY?

Bowser (offstage)
WOW! WOW! WOW!

Sally

Thanks Bowser. So they're real lookers, both of them.

Gary (offstage)

How can you understand my dog so good?

Sally

I have a way with bright animals, Gary. It's a gift.
Now listen. I authorize you to leave your post. Show
them the grave, take them anywhere they want. Tell
them I'll catch up later.

Gary (offstage)

Will do, Boss Lady.

ACT 3, SCENE 3

(In front of the bakery/general store, 4:30 P.M.)

(Present are Gary, Senora Guerrero, Senorita Guerrero, Helicopter
Pilot,
and Clyde, the Fearless Wolf Hunter)

Clyde

Hey son, you live here?

Gary

Yes sir.

Clyde

My buddies went off to Winchester at around four o'clock. How
long would it take them to get there?

                    Gary
What were they driving?

                    Clyde
A Ford 450.

                    Gary
Were they cold sober?

                    Clyde
Sure, I guess so.

                    Gary
Well, then they should make it by six.

                    Clyde
Six o'clock? It's only forty-three miles! And they need to
get there by five to get the licenses.

                    Gary
You couldn't make Winchester by five in a Maserati and
live to tell the tale. Highway 61 has lots of double hairpin turns.
If they tried too hard, I'll be seeing them later.

                    Clyde
You the town mechanic?

                    Gary
No, I'm with the cemetery district.

                    Santini (the Pilot)
Clyde, this gig is finished. You guys were supposed to fly out
at four. That was the contract. Not only that, you never warned
us it was a hunting contract. You have to pay extra for those, it's
hazardous duty.

                    Clyde
How come? Do the wolves shoot back or somethin'?

Senora Guerrero
I hire you now. To see the Mountain of the Brujas. Here is plastic.

(She hands credit card to pilot)

Santini
Ma'am, you need to make a reservation with the office.

Gary
Are you a flyboy or paper pusher?

Senora Guerrero
Here is my reservation Senor.

(She pulls out a Glock)

Gary
I think you want to let this grieving widow see where her husband died on Witch Mountain, Skypilot. Mrs. Guerrero, put the gun back in your purse. It's okay to have one here but it's bad manners to intimidate people with it in public.

Senorita Guerrero
Caramba mi madre. No es pendejo. You're one little brave hombre, Gary. Mom, put it away. This little guy has cojones, and he's real cute.

Santini
Let's fly boys and girls. Paperwork later. Santini will get you there!

ACT 3, SCENE 4

(Dogpatch Kitchen Supply Room, 7:00 P.M.)

(Present are Sally, Charley, Margo)

Sally

Anybody seen Gary? Can't find him anywhere.

Margo

Saw him getting into a helicopter with two ladies dressed in black.

Sally

Gary in a helicopter?

Charley

Riding with witches?

Sally

No love. Ladies in mourning. Mrs. and Miz Guerrero. I'll bet they're heading for Witch Mountain. He sure followed my orders. Smart young man.

Margo

The WOC (Wallamootka Observer Corps) is organized. Made a badge using a photo of a snarling wolverine as our logo.

Charley

And I've advised the helicopter companies by email of our new city anti-aerial hunting statute.

Sally

Hope you reminded them our city limits extend 13 miles outward in each direction from Snowtop to the rim of the

Cascades, and informed them no one can board a helicopter
in the city limits carrying rifles, machine guns, shotguns,
assault rifles, or compound bows with hunting arrows.

Charley
Of course, Sweetheart. And "Cave Man" hunters using
homemade bows, and flint or obsidian-tipped arrowheads
and spears are exempt from these provisions.

Sally
Right! We leave opportunity for today's real sportsmen.

Margo
All our watchers have binoculars, cameras, radios, and cell
phones and are heading out in various directions. The telescope-
camera is over on the small knoll above the lake where it can
sweep the high peaks. On a clear day you can even see Mt.
Trump, unless it is sending up hot gases. Only semi-dormant
volcanic peak in the county. And there's Politician Peak, the bane
of rock climbers because it has two false tops.

Sally
Let's do dinner. Steaks for everyone. Everything's on the
house tonight.

ACT 3, SCENE 5

(In front of the bakery/general store, 10:00 P.M.)

(Sally and Charley exit the back door of the Dogpatch Saloon and walk
in front of the bakery/general store)

Sally
I need some air. What a day! Look at all those stars coming out,
Charley.

Charley

Yeah, city folk don't know what they're missing. By the way,
how's Miz Guerrero working out as a specialty cook? You've
had her on staff now for six weeks.

Sally

Outstanding. The tourists love her carne asada and empanadas.
And she does Szechuan too. She speaks English, Spanish,
Spanglish, Arabic, Quechua, and Mapuche! Imagine that! It was
nice of her mother to donate the mini-park behind the general
store, and the bronze statue of Wallamootka. Gives the town a
center. She was so thrilled I gave her back her husband's crucifix
before she even asked for it. He was a Catholic after all, baptized
as Cristoforo Pablo Guerrero but changed his first names in
honor of Mrs. Guerrero's uncle, who helped them elope from
Saudi Arabia and paid with his life. His new names helped
him to sound more ferocious to his competitors. The macho
thing.

Charley

Ain't life strange!

Sally

And Gary told me how Miz Guerrero's parents met. It was in a
remote place in the Middle East called Uyun al-Hammam.
Mrs. Guerrero was educated in a sort of convent/university for
rich girls in Madrid. So she spoke Spanish and was an
archaeology major. Seeing remote archaeological sites was Mr.
Guerrero's hobby. So that's how their life paths crossed.

Charley

I think I've read about this place. Wasn't it in Jordan? And it has
the oldest known cemetery in the Middle East. It's over sixteen
thousand years old!

Sally

That's right Charley. And Gary was impressed to pieces by that.
In the older part was buried a red fox with the people corpses,
somebody's pet or hunting companion. And later dogs as well.

Charley

And to think we've only been burying people and pets here since 1857.

(Clyde enters, waves to his four fearless wolf-hunter buddies offstage)

Clyde

Hurry up and pee, you guys, I've found the town hooker.
Let's have some fun.

Charley

At ease, Dirtbag. You're looking at the owner of Dogpatch and half the town. Just because she looks like a Turkish belly dancer is no reason to slander a lady. She was born a looker—a problem you don't have, I can see.

Clyde

You her brother or something?

Charley

You might say that.

Clyde

Bet you'd rather be her sweetheart.

Charley

Not really. Her husband, yes.

Clyde

I think you're pulling my leg little man. Go away. I think you're her pimp and you're gassing and sassing with me to drive the price up. Like the oil companies did to the price of gas. Can't hardly drive my truck anywhere without I get a loan. Have to ask my buddies to chip in for the gas. That sucks.

Charley

I can see you're not totally devoid of sense. Maybe you city fellas have different ways but out here in the boonies this is still

Louis L'Amour country and insults to our womenfolk are taken seriously. But we can make allowances for outsiders who don't know our ways. So why don't you simply apologize to Sally and put this little tiff behind us right now?

Clyde
And who might you be, the Lone Ranger without your mask?

Charley
The town's legal counsel. And Sally's been my friend for fifteen years. That lady in the general store window (pointing offstage) is the Justice of the Peace; she's on the phone with the chief of police right now.

Clyde
I still think you're pulling my leg. Making a sharp bluff.

Charley
We'll see you. We're going across the way to the park.

Clyde
We'll be seeing you too.

(Sally and Charley exit first, followed by Clyde)

Mabel (offstage)
Phil, get over to the park; a bunch of roughnecks are harassing Sally and Charley.

Phil (offstage)
Are they in for a surprise!

Mabel (offstage)
Oops. Sally just flipped that Clyde fellow. A hip throw it was. He landed hard. Charley's clobbered two of them. Lucky the others don't know much about fighting. Wow! Sally just elbowed two of them in the breadbasket. Here's Phil.
It's all over.

(Charley and Sally walk back in front of the bakery/general store, followed sheepishly by Clyde)

Clyde
Ma'am, I apologize most sincerely. I was way wrong about you.

(He offers Sally a handshake and she accepts.)

Sally
Apology accepted. Next time visit Mustang Ranch in Nevada when your hormones and those of your friends go into overdrive. See Adriana and tell her I sent you. She was a dorm-mate of mine at college.

Clyde
Thanks, sport!

Sally
And we do have a town prostitute but she only sees locals. When she doesn't have her shingle out, like now, she shacks up with some guy for a while. Whether she's a business woman or a house frau, she's one of us! Snowtop's city statutes don't forbid the oldest profession. But pimps get tarred and feathered here, and worse if they deserve it.

Clyde
No kidding!

(Clyde waves goodbye and exits)

Charley
I guess they didn't know us country hicks were both Fourth Dan black belts.

Sally
Not likely. City folk think we're rubes. I'm glad my dad made me learn this stuff.

Charley
Me too. Oh, by the way Sally, would you marry me?

Sally
Of course. Been waiting five years. You're different all of
a sudden.

Charley
It's the book the chief gave me about the wolverine way.
It's inspired me. I want to be a Wallamootka human instead
of a rabbit human. Maybe I'll open a dojo here to help
rabbits become Wallamootkas. Gotta borrow from East and West
to find our way to a better future.

Sally
Good, otherwise I would have come prowlin' after you next
Sadie Hawkins day.

(They embrace and smooch)

ACT 3, SCENE 6

(The mine on Witch Mountain, a bright crisp October morning)

(Present are Gary, Sally, Bowser, Chief Joseph, Mabel, and Senorita
Guerrero)

Gary
Hey look, there's a helicopter coming.

Sally
But it's not due until 4:00. Maybe there's a front moving in.

Bowser

Waughter! Waughter!

Gary

Why you want water, dog? You had a drink ten minutes ago.

Chief Joseph

No. He's saying Walter. It's a DEA bird. I see Walter waving
at us and an older guy driving.

Gary

You speak dog talk too, Chief?

Chief Joseph

Sure, and English too.

(Helicopter lands)

(Walter enters and points offstage)

Walter

Hi gang! This is my boss, Casper. Mind if he just pokes
around on his own? He loves to visit weird crime scenes
after reading about them in my reports.

Sally

Help yourself Casper.

Walter

Sorry I couldn't be at the wedding. Had to go to Afghanistan.
Can't trust anybody over there these days. Almost didn't come
back at all. They've got it into their heads we've started the Fifth
Crusade and without even getting the Pope's blessing first.
And bin Laden transfigured from live cheerleader/recruiter to
dead hero/martyr.

(Sally hugs Walter)

Sally

Welcome home partner. Thanks for sending me all those books
and clippings. Couldn't have got the old mine running without
you. Last week's gross ore meltdown exceeded fifteen grand.

Mabel

First two weeks barely netted twenty, but everybody in town has
paid off their accounts at the general store and their bar tabs at
Dogpatch. So Herbert and I feel we can now stock lots more stuff
at the store and invest in Luke Lagomarsino's ice wine project.
Same thing happened to this town once before. My parents
extended credit to folks at the store during the Depression, till
they were flat broke. Banker Stevens in Winchester took the
risk of giving all of us a line of credit. As the first social security
checks started coming, old people started paying off their store
tabs and the bank got repaid. The youngsters had gone away to
two world wars to make the world safe for something or other.
Of those who survived few wanted to come back here, until they
tired of the big city.

Walter

These out of the way little towns like yours may be the salvation
of humankind and civilization if someone is ever foolish enough
to press the nuclear button. These politicians that have rekindled
the Cold War worry me.

Mabel

Everyone in town that has more than six quarters, does business
with dowdy old Winchester Savings and Loan, where Priscilla
knows all her customers on sight. And Sally's granddad, Abner
Jones, is mainly responsible for its survival, because in the
Depression he refused to pull out any of his savings when others
were in panic. He said if it wasn't safe in Steven's bank it wasn't
safe anywhere anyhow. There was never a run on Winchester
Savings so we all survived. To this town and the entire county
of Winchester, Abner's like Robert Morris was to the American
Revolution. Folks here don't fuss over the stock market's
conniptions nor worry what flavor flu virus is coming around

next year. They're too busy surviving day-to-day.

                              Sally
Walt, the job of mine superintendent is open for you anytime you
retire. When you're not up here you'll have a permanent room at
the hotel.

                              Walter
Thanks! Say, how did you get all these people in here? They don't
look like they could make the hike.

                              Mabel
Charley did it. Made a compromise with the helicopter rental
company. We caught them red-handed on your telescope-camera.
Flying wolf hunters in illegally. Instead of paying the steep fine
they agreed to ferry us in and out a few times. In the meantime,
they've spotted where the animals can be seen and where the
spectacular views are. Now they run nature tour flights and give
us low rates to freight our miners in and out.

                              Walter
Thanks for the job offer, but maybe I could just buy a house or a
lot here instead.

                              Bowser
WA! WA! WA!

                              Sally
Bowser's laughing at you Walter because you don't know all this
place's surprises yet. There hasn't been any property in town for
sale for a hundred and twenty-seven years. Ninety years ago the
town enacted a no-growth ordnance because we believe we've
reached the maximum carrying capacity of this valley. We have
no sewers and no treated water. Don't want them, don't need
them, can't afford them. We know biology though; we marry
outside the valley. For instance, Charley's from Winchester.
                              Walter
Remarkable! In effect you've set limits to human population

growth in your town based on septic field capacity. And reigned in urban sprawl as well. You have built-in social distancing; you all have lots of house and yard space. Achievements worthy of note by some committee or other of the U.N.

Senorita Guerrero
Caramba mi madre. As an outsider I thought I could never...

(Swivels her head to stare at Gary and smiles)

(Bowser stands erect)

Bowser
Little Dude, run! Don't look back or you'll be changed to salt. Your last chance is to hike out of here now and join the government's Foreign Legion or the Red Cross's Japanese Earthquake Relief Corps. Or maybe Greenpeace.

(Bowser lies back down)

Sally
Did you hear we had some trouble with your FBI buddies on the Fourth of July?

Walter
Not a thing! Tell me about it.

Sally
Seems Chester's boss was real unhappy with the loss of their telescope-camera. More so because Gary's claim, supported by Mabel's decision, is wending its way through the Washington State court system. So Chester tried to 'steal back' the telescope-camera. On his own or under orders, we don't know.

Walter
He did? Wouldn't have believed him capable of pulling off a caper like that.
Sally
We think he twisted Tiffany's arm into helping him. It was her

planning that got the rental van halfway up Highway 61 before we knew what happened.

Walter
No way! How did you stop them?

Sally
The bush telegraph—and luck. Chief Joseph called his shepherds, Pedro and Carlos, who had just crossed the highway near the top with the flock, in one of the few spots of cellular reception. Carlos spotted the van coming and Pedro cut down an eight inch diameter tree with an axe in sixty seconds, blocking the highway.

Charley
Phil pulled up behind them with flashing lights and following the script Mayor Shorty gave him, told them to return their cargo and no official notice would be made of the matter.

Sally
That saved our summer eco-tourism. That telescope-camera is a crowd pleaser.

Mabel
One tiny mystery remains. When Phil pulled up, Chester was alone in the van claiming he had pulled off the job himself. And mumbling about people off in the woods, chattering away in some dumb foreign language he'd never heard before. Then Tiff showed up ten minutes later looking pretty bedraggled, saying she lost her way after taking a potty break.

Charley
Nice of him to cover for Tiffany.
(Mabel faces the audience)

Mabel
I wonder if that foreign language was Basque. What do you think?

Walter
That's an amazing story you just told me. And you people are the
ecological cutting-edge. Way ahead of your time. Tell me about
this ice wine. Had some in Germany.

Mabel
Luke took ice wine vines and crossed them with 'stinkum' bushes-
plants that are natural pesticides, so all varmints large and small
would leave it alone. Won first prize at the California State Fair.
Here's what the wine judge said.

(Mable pulls paper from her pocket)

Mable (continues)
"As Napoleon advised drinking Chambertin on your knees, with
your hat off, I advise drinking this wine while wearing a wool
sweater and cap. It will paralyze your palate and give your sinuses
an arctic blast coming across the tops of the Cascade Mountains."

Walter
That sounds really promising Mabel. Sally, did you ever find out
what your grandpa originally named this mine?

Sally
You really won't believe…The Lucky Witch Mountain
Wallamootka Mine.

ALL
(including CHORUS)
(with both clenched fists raised in salute)

LONG LIVE THE WALLAMOOTKA!

CURTAIN AND FINIS